WORLD IN  D

AIR

Steve Pollock

Illustrated by Peter Wingham

Belitha Press

First published in Great Britain in 1990 by
Belitha Press Limited
31 Newington Green, London N16 9PU

Text copyright © Steve Pollock 1990
Illustrations copyright © Peter Wingham 1990
Editor: Neil Champion

All rights reserved. No part of this book may be reproduced
or utilised in any form or by any means, electronic or
mechanical, including photocopying, recording or by any
information storage and retrieval system, without
permission in writing from the publisher.

ISBN 1-85561-033-7

Printed in the UK by MacLehose for Imago Publishing
Printed on recycled paper (132 gsm envirocote)

Contents

The air in balance	4
Something in the air	6
Polluted air	8
When did it all start?	10
Cars and pollution	12
The world is getting warmer	14
The ozone layer	16
Acid rain	18
Nuclear power	20
Noise pollution	22
Climate and weather	24
Air pollution action	26
Air fact file	28
Further information	30
Glossary	31
Index	32

The air in balance

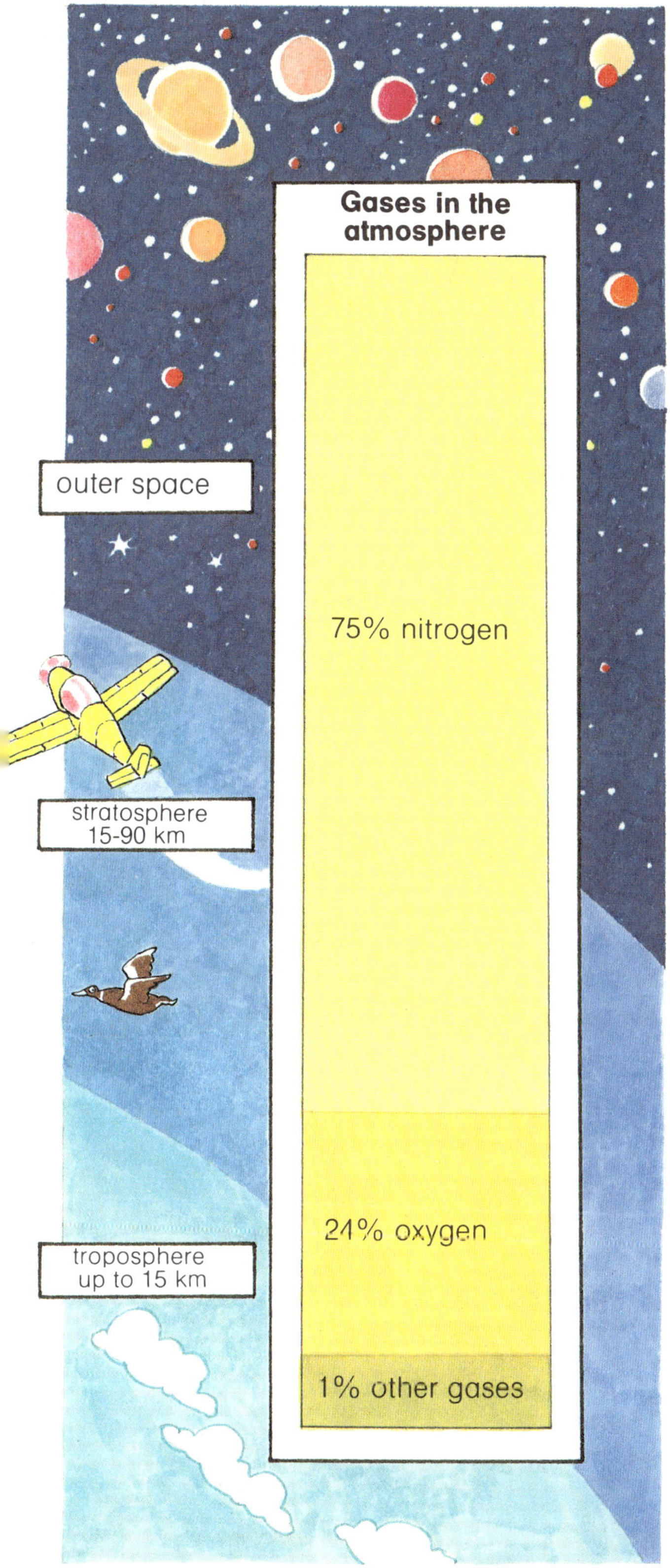

Gases in the atmosphere

- outer space
- stratosphere 15-90 km
- troposphere up to 15 km

- 75% nitrogen
- 24% oxygen
- 1% other gases

The Earth is the only planet in our **solar system** that has life. One of the things which makes life possible is our **atmosphere**. It contains **oxygen**, which all plants and animals need.

When we breathe we take oxygen into our lungs, which then passes into the bloodstream. The blood takes oxygen to different parts of our body. When we breathe out we remove **carbon dioxide**. We also remove water which on a cold day you can see as a fine mist.

There are two main layers in the atmosphere. The **troposphere** and the **stratosphere**.

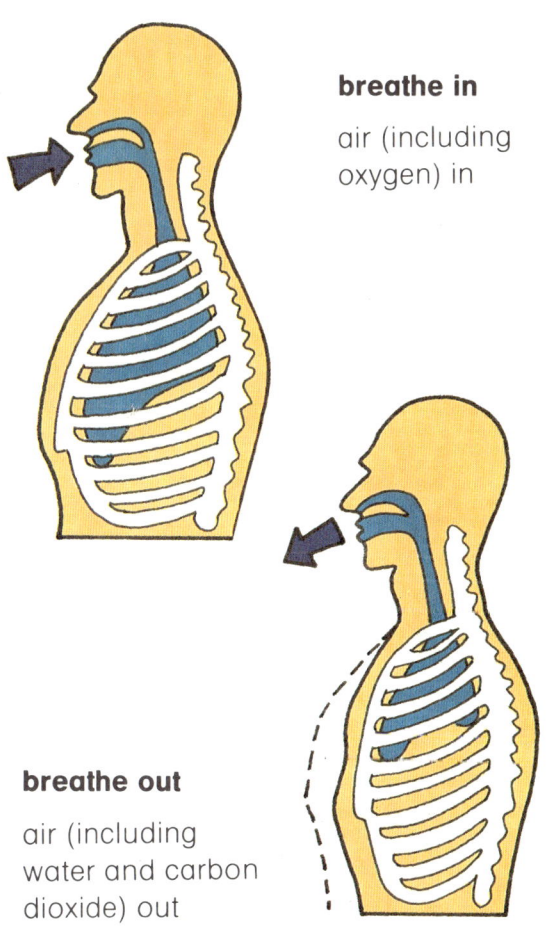

breathe in

air (including oxygen) in

breathe out

air (including water and carbon dioxide) out

Something in the air

Nearly all living things need oxygen for breathing, including plants. Those animals that breathe air have lungs. Which of the animals below breathe air? They all do! The crocodile lives on land and water. It has special flaps on its nose to stop water getting into its lungs.

The whale is an air-breather too even though it lives in the sea. Its nostril is on top of its head. When it comes to the surface it breathes through its nostril, or blowhole. Whales can hold their breath for a long time. Water-breathing animals (like fish, lobsters and shrimps) have **gills** not lungs. The water spider lives under the water but breathes air. Like a **scuba diver** it takes a bubble of air down under water with it. The bubble acts as a kind of lung too. Oxygen from the water passes into the bubble, helping the spider to stay under longer.

air-breathing animals

Each leaf of a plant is an oxygen factory. They use sunlight and the gas carbon dioxide which the plant turns into oxygen. This chemical reaction is called **photosynthesis**. All plants do this when the Sun is shining. Even the tiny microscopic plants called phytoplankton do this.

The roots of trees and plants take in water and goodness from soil.

Polluted air

Can you see some of the ways in which the air is being polluted in this city? In London in the 1950s, **smog** killed over 4,000 people. From that time on, laws have helped cut down the amount of smoke and dirt in the air.

People smoking cigarettes, pipes and cigars make the air unhealthy for others nearby. What's worse is that people can get diseases as a result of breathing the

air polluted by smokers. More and more public places are banning smoking. This helps keep the air cleaner.

The air is full of germs. Most of the time they do not bother us. Sometimes though, other people cough and sneeze and send germs flying our way.

Some of the chemicals we use can create air pollution too. Hair sprays, and chemicals in the kitchen and bathroom can all throw harmful material into the air.

Sometimes the air in the countryside stops being fresh and clean. In some countries, farmers burn the stalks of crops after harvesting. This fouls the air with smoke and greasy smuts.

When did it all start?

People probably first started polluting the air when they learnt how to make fire. In those days there were so few people on the Earth that the smoke could not have done much harm. The first harmful pollution started in Great Britain with the arrival of the **Industrial Revolution**.

With the change from burning wood to burning coal came huge changes in people's way of life. People moved from working in the fields to working in factories.

The peppered moth population even changed colour. Sooty smoke made the trees dark, which meant that the white moths showed up. These were easily caught by birds. The few dark moths in the population survived. Eventually few white ones were left so that there were now mainly dark ones in the population. Since the **Clean Air Act** was passed in 1956, the air in Great Britain is much less smoky.

Cars and pollution

One of the worst kinds of pollution comes from the motor car. There are over half a billion vehicles around the world all making some kind of pollution. The exhaust fumes from cars are unpleasant and dangerous.

Cars that run on **leaded petrol** create a problem. They throw lead into the air which can end up in the bloodstream in children. It then quickly gets into their brain. Children who have a lot of lead in their body can become sick.

In Los Angeles, cars make so much pollution that it can cause smog.

The exhaust fumes from cars cough out the following chemicals into the air:

- Carbon monoxide – this is a poisonous gas when there is a lot of it about in a small space. It also causes certain kinds of smog.
- Hydrocarbons – there are hundreds of different kinds coming out of car exhaust pipes. Some may cause cancer.
- Nitrogen oxides – they can cause diseases such as bronchitis and pneumonia. They also cause acid rain.
- Carbon dioxide – the main gas which adds to the greenhouse effect.

In Japan pollution is so bad that there are oxygen machines on the street.

A new European Law will mean all cars built after 1992 will have to be fitted with a three-way **catalytic converter**. In parts of the USA many of the cars already have catalytic converters. A catalytic converter helps cut down the amount of polluting gases which come out of the car's exhaust. Using unleaded petrol helps to cut down the lead which gets into the air from car exhausts.

People have tried building non-polluting cars. This is a small car designed to run on electricity from batteries.

catalytic converter

There are other less polluting ways of getting around. Using a bike is healthy and does not create pollution.

Walking rather than driving is healthier for you, the air and your dog!

The world is getting warmer

The Earth is heated by the Sun. Much of this heat warms everything on the Earth's surface. Some of this heat from the Earth is lost back into the air and then disappears into space.

Certain gases such as carbon dioxide hold onto the heat. When there is too much carbon dioxide the Earth gets warmer. In recent years more carbon dioxide has been made because of burning coal and trees, and cars producing exhaust fumes.

A warmer Earth will cause the ice in the Arctic and Antarctic to melt. A piece the size of Wales has already broken away from the main Antarctic sheet.

This will raise the sea levels so that many of the world's islands and low lying places will disappear under water forever.

Some people think that the sea level is rising by 8 mm every year. In 50 years time this could cause problems for us all. Many people will lose their homes and will need to live somewhere else. Countries such as Bangladesh and the Netherlands would very quickly become flooded. Where will all those millions of people live?

The change in the world's temperatures may mean that places which now grow one kind of crop may no longer be able to.

We must all work together to stop adding more to the **greenhouse effect**.

Some ways of helping

stop wasting energy

stop cutting down trees

stop using cars unnecessarily

The ozone layer

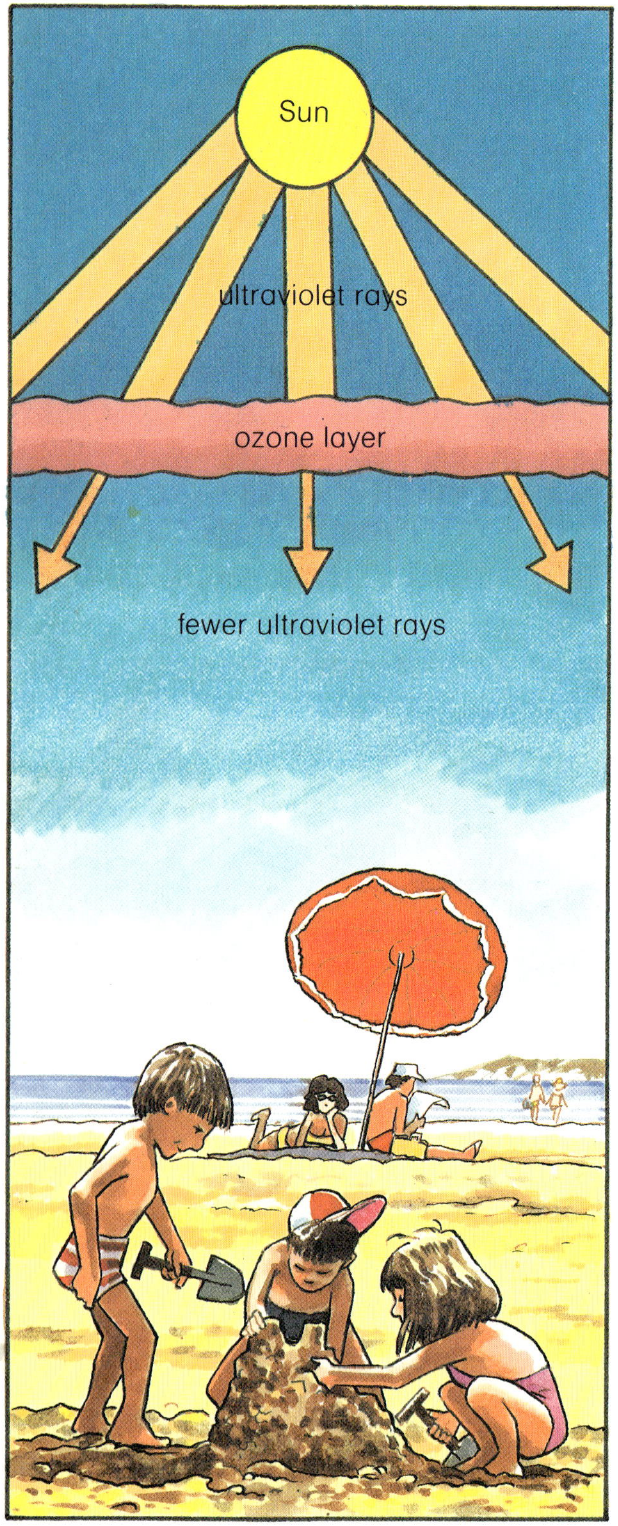

High above the Earth is a layer of gas called the **ozone**. This ozone layer cuts down the amount of ultraviolet rays from the Sun. These are the rays that can burn our skin.

We now know there is some danger for us all from these rays because we are polluting the air with chemicals which damage the ozone layer. Chemicals called **CFCs** are used in aerosol sprays, refrigerators, air conditioning units and to make expanded polystyrene.

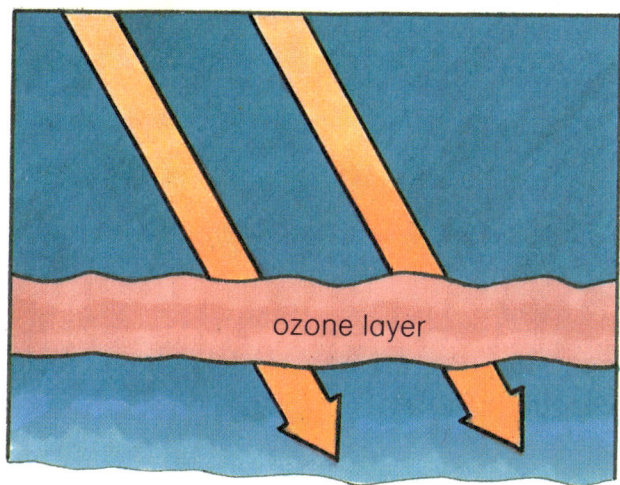

CFCs cause a chemical reaction which destroys ozone. Holes and patches appear in the ozone layer. A large patch appears over the South Pole and the North Pole every spring.

This means that more ultraviolet rays will pass through the ozone and reach the Earth. Ultraviolet radiation causes sunburn, eye damage and skin cancer. It may interfere with the way some seeds and plants grow. This could create problems for us all. Those people living near the South Pole (for example, in Australia) will have to take special care when they are out in the sun.

The good news is that many companies have stopped using CFCs. Many countries have also agreed to reduce the amount they produce.

Acid rain

Smoke from burning coal contains chemicals. These chemicals get into the air and cause pollution. One chemical in the smoke is sulphur dioxide. When this chemical mixes with water it turns it into a very weak acid. Can you think what happens when the smoke mixes with rain? The rain reacts with the sulphur dioxide and becomes slightly acid. We call this acid rain. Mostly acid rain is weaker than vinegar, so it does not harm our skin or bodies.

Acid rain can cause trees and plants to become sick. It may turn ponds and lakes slightly acid.

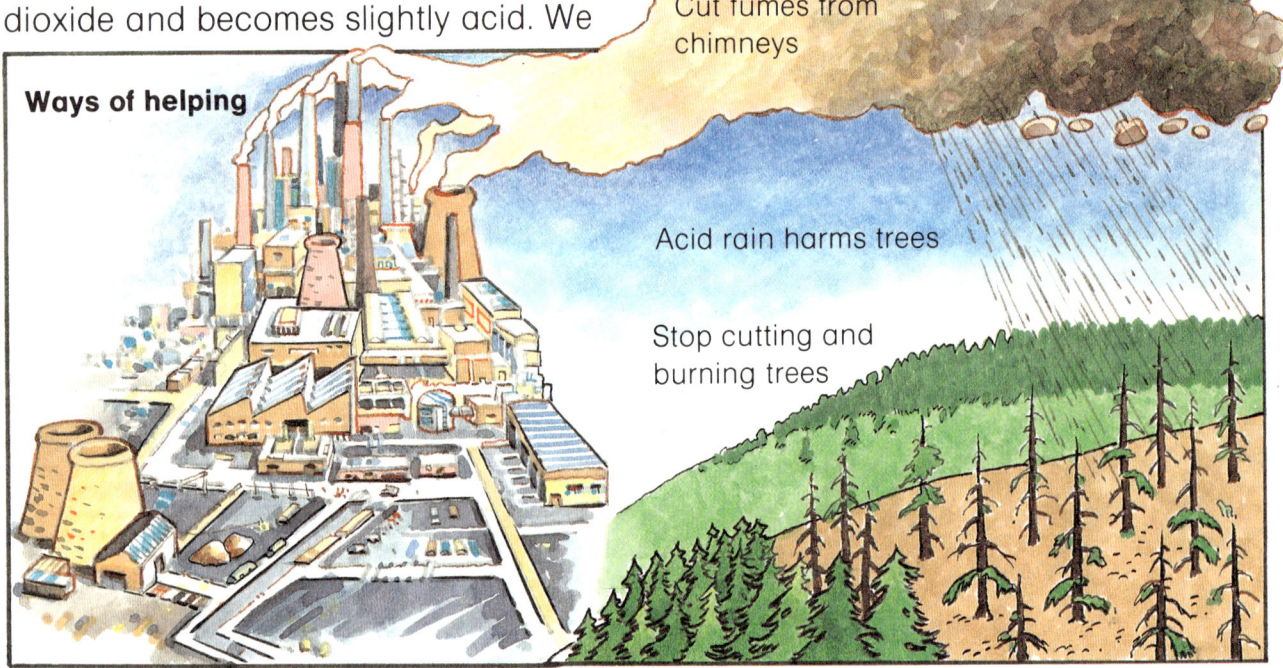

Ways of helping

Cut fumes from chimneys

Acid rain harms trees

Stop cutting and burning trees

This man is making a fire

The smoke from the fire pollutes another person's home

An ancient Greek building attacked by acid rain

A dipper – acid rain kills the insects it lives on

Acid rain also harms buildings. It can eat into marble and chalky stone and wear them away.

One of the main problems with acid rain is who causes the pollution in the first place. Some European countries are blaming other countries for creating acid rain. It's a bit like the two men on the islands. Wind blows polluting smoke from one place to another.

There are ways to reduce the amount of acid rain falling. Special equipment called gas scrubbers can be fitted to chimneys pouring out smoke. These help to remove the sulphur that causes acid rain. Catalytic converters can be fitted to car exhausts. This reduces the amount of polluting gases, which can also make acid rain. Today more effort is being made to cut down the pollution that causes acid rain.

Chalky lime is sometimes added to lakes in the hope of stopping water turning acid.

Nuclear power

In April 1986 a terrible accident happened in Russia. The nuclear power station at Chernobyl blew up. In a nuclear power station energy is created along with radioactivity. Normally the radioactive part is kept under control.

At Chernobyl it took ten days to stop the energy and radioactivity from being made after the accident.

In that time a radioactive cloud blew across into western Europe. The rain was polluted with radioactivity. This caused problems for those people living there. The soil and vegetation became polluted. Reindeer which are herded in Lapland and Finland could not be sold for meat. They were too polluted, too radioactive for people to eat. The same was true of sheep in parts of Great Britain.

Radioactive objects give off radiation. There is a lot of radiation in nature. A kind of rock called granite is radioactive. It gives off radiation. The problem happens when too much radiation is given off. When radiation passes into our bodies, it can damage our cells. This can sometimes cause cancer.

After Chernobyl people realised that nuclear power stations might not be as safe as we had thought.

Coal, oil, gas and nuclear power are all called non-renewable ways of making energy. That's because once all the

to be done to find the ideal renewable source of energy. The quicker we find it the quicker we cut down pollution.

coal, oil, gas and **uranium** are used up there is nothing left. So people are looking at other ways to make energy.

Solar panels use the heat of the Sun. Wind turbines use the power of the wind to make energy. All these are renewable sources of energy because they will not run out. They are also clean. There is much research left

sun's rays

Noise pollution

Something we don't often think about in the air is noise pollution. Look carefully at this picture of life in a town. Can you see who might be making the noises and what they might be like? Some noises are important, others are dangerous. Why do you think this is?

Climate and weather

Weather is one of the most important things happening in the air. It controls the way we live. Some people think the weather is changing: the world is getting warmer. Some people think that pollution is to blame.

Others think that the weather changes anyway. Weather was thought to have been warmer when the Romans lived in Britain. During the 1600s and 1700s there was a cold period in Britain called the 'little ice age'. It got so cold that the River Thames froze over every winter.

Scientists think that the reason dinosaurs died out was because the weather changed. Somehow dust

Keeping an eye on the weather is quite easy to do with simple equipment. You can make a rain gauge using the top and bottom of a plastic fizzy drink bottle. Use the base to hold the rain. Cut the top off and turn it upside down onto the bottom to collect the rain. It can act as a kind of funnel.

Measure wind speed using a home-made yogurt pot **anemometer**. You will need to count the number of turns to decide the wind speed. Make a wind direction finder. Use a compass to find out where North is. Make the arm of the direction finder loose enough to move around easily. Keep a weather notebook. See if the weather forecasters got it right for the area you live in!

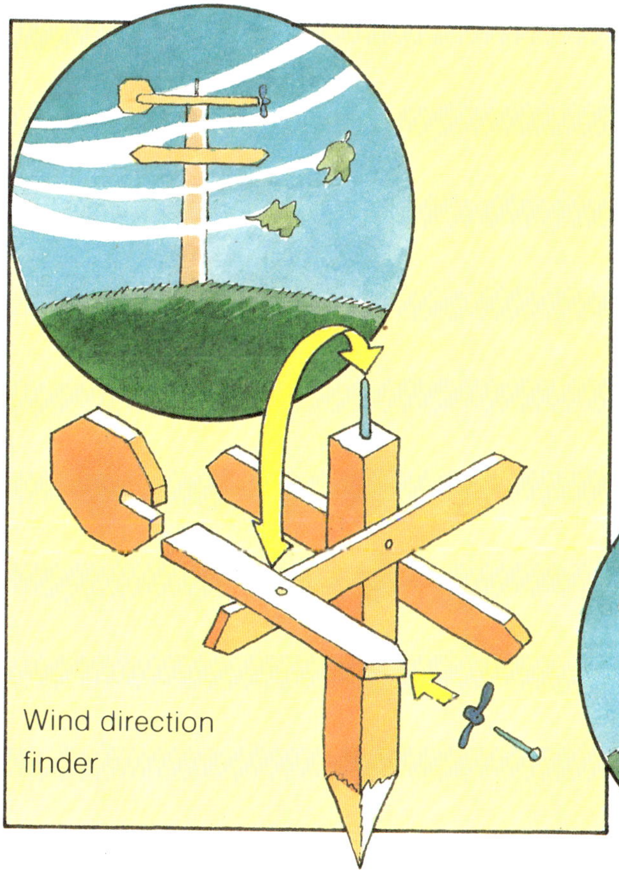

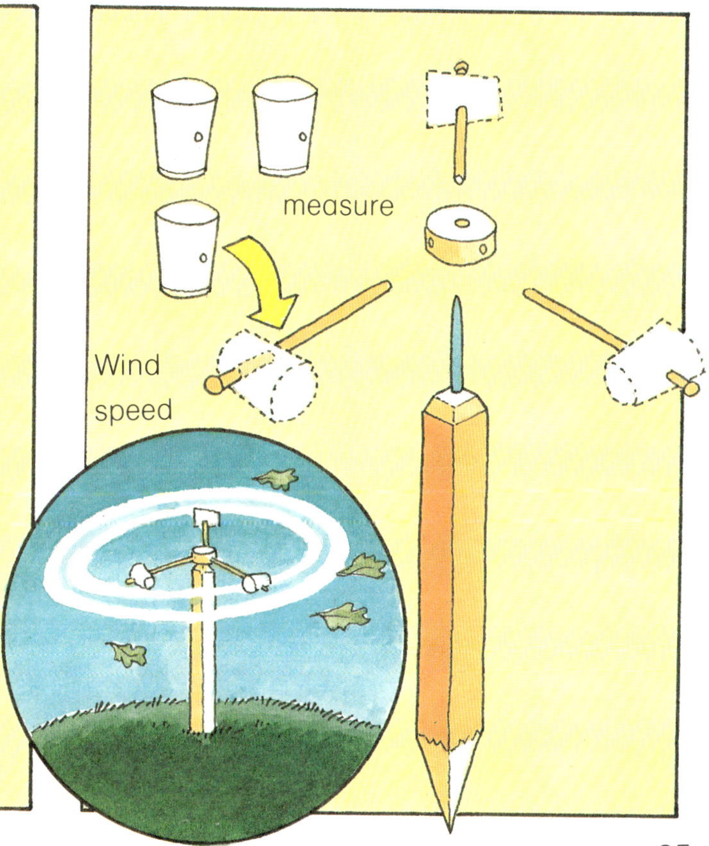

particles got into the air and stopped the Sun from warming up the Earth. The dinosaurs couldn't cope with this and they died out.

Wind direction finder

measure

Wind speed

Air pollution action

Because there are so many invisible things floating in the air, special ways have to be used to discover what's there and whether it is harmful or not.

People have used many different methods. They have also studied the world around them to give them clues. Nature itself can tell us how healthy our air is. Here are a few examples.

The air in coalmines can be dangerous. It is caused by a poisonous gas. In the past, coalminers used canaries to let them know that gas was close by. If the canary breathed the gas it would stop singing and die. This saved the miner who would quickly escape from the gas. Today, special equipment is used to detect this poisonous gas.

This special equipment is also used to measure the level of poisonous chemicals in our atmosphere. A **Geiger counter** is used to measure radio-activity, for example.

A canary – used to detect gases in coalmines

You can find out how polluted the air is in an area by looking carefully at special plants called lichens. If the air is polluted there will be very few lichens. When the air is clean there are many different kinds. Look closely and you will see some that spread over quite a large area. Others have tall cup-shaped parts to them. Where you find these varieties the air is quite healthy.

A good place to look for lichens is on gravestones. Check the dates on the stones. Are the older ones covered with more lichens than the newer ones?

Lichen – a sign of clean air

But sometimes we can use simple equipment to measure pollution. Put a white coffee filter paper, or blotting paper, outside. After a while measure the amount of dirt collected on the paper.

Lichen on gravestones

Air fact file

Holes in the ozone

The ozone layer stops too much ultraviolet light from reaching the Earth's surface.

Each spring in the Antarctic a hole appears in the ozone layer. It can be as big as the USA. When this happens more ultraviolet light reaches the Earth through this hole. We know that this extra ultraviolet light will cause damage to living things. It will increase the chance of eye and skin diseases in people. Fortunately every summer the hole over the Antarctic closes up and the ozone layer is complete once again.

Thin Air

Most of the Earth's oxygen is found quite close to the Earth's surface. The higher you go the less oxygen there is available. When climbers climb up a mountain, they need to take an extra supply of oxygen with them because at the top, there is not enough oxygen for them to breathe. This happens on very high mountains.

Planting trees

Some countries such as Holland are thinking about replacing forests in tropical countries. This is to balance out the burning of coal in some of their power stations. When coal is burned, the carbon from the plants of which it is made gets into the atmosphere as carbon dioxide. This extra carbon dioxide creates problems in global warming. The extra carbon dioxide made by burning will be used up by the extra trees that will be planted and so balance will be restored.

Nature recycles

There is more nitrogen in our atmosphere than any other gas; but there is very little carbon dioxide (although the amount is increasing). However, both these gases are very important for living things. Plants take the carbon dioxide and use it for growing. Special bacteria turn the gas into a chemical which plants can use. The carbon and nitrogen pass into living things and are returned into the air. This keeps happening over again in a constant cycle of use and reuse.

The atmosphere

When the Earth was very young (about 4.2 billion years ago) the atmosphere was very different from the one we know today. Probably 80% of the air was made of water vapour. About 12% was carbon dioxide, 7% sulphur dioxide and 1% nitrogen. It was the very early microscopic plants that made the oxygen we now breathe. Without these plants using sunlight and carbon dioxide in the air there would be no oxygen. It took about 2.5 billion years before there was enough oxygen to allow other forms of life to appear on Earth.

A heat wave

In 1984, a heat wave in Athens created a very dangerous smog. The drivers of half the private cars in the city were told they were not allowed to drive for two days. Industries had to cut down their fuel consumption so they did not make so much smoke. About 500 people were taken to hospital because they were having problems breathing. Athens suffers very badly from air pollution.

Global warning

If countries cannot agree to do something about global warming soon, the sea will have risen 45 cm by the year 2070. This would mean many people living in low-lying areas would be in danger of losing their homes from flooding.

Further information

There are many organisations involved with helping nature and our environment. Below are the addresses of just some of the more well known ones that you may like to contact. They may also be able to put you in touch with local organisations, if you want to get actively involved with things such as fund-raising through sponsored events. Remember, our natural world needs every friend and helper it can get!

Friends of the Earth
26-28 Underwood Street
London N1 7JQ

World Wide Fund for Nature
Panda House
Weyside Park
Godalming
Surrey GU7 1XR

British Trust for Nature Conservation
    Volunteers
36 St Mary's Street
Wallingford
Oxfordshire OX10 0EU

Greenpeace
30-31 Islington Green
London N1 8XT

The Conservation Trust
George Palmer Site
Northumberland Avenue
Reading
Berkshire RG2 7PW

Royal Society for the Protection of
    Birds
The Lodge
Sandy
Bedfordshire

The People's Trust for Endangered
    Species
Hamble House
Meadrow
Godalming
Surrey GU7 3JX

Glossary

Anemometer A machine that measures the wind, its direction, speed and force.

Atmosphere The mix of gases that surround a planet. We call Earth's atmosphere, the air.

Carbon dioxide One of the ingredients of the air that surrounds us. We breathe out carbon dioxide and so do all other animals. It has no colour or smell.

Catalytic converter A small stainless steel box placed in the exhaust of a car. It changes harmful chemicals given off by a car's engine, into water, carbon dioxide and nitrogen.

CFCs (chlorofluorocarbons) Gases used in industry which damage the ozone layer.

Clean Air Act This was a law passed in Britain in 1956. It helped control the amount of smoke from factories and houses in towns and cities.

Geiger counter A machine that detects and measures radioactivity, named after a physicist, Hans Geiger (1882-1947).

Gills Animals that live in water have gills which enable them to breathe. Gills take oxygen from the water just as our lungs take oxygen from the air we breathe.

Greenhouse effect The warming up of the Earth due to the blanketing effect of man-made carbon dioxide in the air.

Industrial Revolution The change from working in the home, in a 'cottage industry', to many people working in factories 'mass producing' a large number of goods.

Leaded petrol Petrol that still contains lead which is harmful to the environment and the atmosphere.

Oxygen 24% of air is made up of oxygen. It cannot be seen or smelt and is vital to life in all forms on Earth.

Ozone layer One of the outer gas layers of the Earth's atmosphere. It is important because it catches harmful ultraviolet rays that the Sun gives off.

Photosynthesis Green plants make food for themselves out of carbon dioxide and water with the help of energy from the Sun's rays. This is photosynthesis.

Scuba diver A diver who uses a piece of equipment called a scuba – **S**elf-**C**ontained **U**nderwater **B**reathing **A**pparatus.

Smog A combination of smoke and fog.

Solar system Principally the nine planets that go around the Sun (including Earth). Meteors, asteroids and comets are also in the Solar system.

Stratosphere A layer of the atmosphere that is 11-24 kilometres above us.

Troposphere This is the nearest part of our atmosphere reaching from the surface of the Earth to 15 kilometres above us.

Uranium A radioactive metal used in a nuclear reactor to make nuclear energy.

Index

Acid rain 18-19
Aerosol spray 16
Anemometer 25
Antarctic 15, 17, 28
Arctic 15, 17
Atmosphere 5, 26, 28, 29
Australia 17

Bacteria 28
Bangladesh 15
Batteries 13
Birds 11
Breathing 5, 6

Canary 26
Cancer 17, 21
Car 12-13, 14, 19
Carbon 28
Carbon dioxide 5, 7, 12, 14, 28-29
Carbon monoxide 12
Catalytic converter 13, 19
Cells 20
CFCs 16-17
Chernobyl 20
Clean Air Act 11
Climate 24
Coal 10, 14, 18, 20, 28
   mines 26
Crocodile 6
Crops 15

Dinosaurs 24
Disease 8, 12, 28

Electricity 13
Energy 20-21
Exhaust fumes 12-13, 14

Finland 20

Fish 6
Floods 15

Gas 7, 14, 16, 20-21, 28
Geiger counter 26
Germs 9
Global warming 14-15, 28-29
Gravestones 27
Great Britain 10-11, 20, 24
Greenhouse effect 15

Hair sprays 9
Holland 29

Industrial Revolution 10
Insects 19

Japan 13

Lapland 20
Lead 12
Leaded petrol 12
Lichens 27
Little ice age 24
Lungs 5, 6

Netherlands 15
Nitrogen 5, 28-29
Nitrogen oxides 12
Nuclear power 20-21

Oil 20-21
Oxygen 5, 6-7, 28, 29
Ozone 16-17, 28

Peppered moth 11
Photosynthesis 7
Phytoplankton 7
Plants 5, 6-7, 18

Pollution 8-9, 10-11, 16-17, 18-19, 24, 26-27, 29
   car 12-13
   measuring 27
   noise 22-23
   nuclear 20-21
Power station 20, 28

Radiation 20
Radioactivity 20, 26
Reindeer 20
River Thames 24
Romans 24
Russia 20

Sea 6, 15, 29
Scuba diver 6
Smog 8, 12, 29
Smoke 9, 10-11, 18-19, 29
Solar panels 21
Solar system 5
Stratosphere 5
Sulphur 19
Sulphur dioxide 18, 29
Sun 7, 14, 16-17, 21, 25

Trees 11, 14 18, 28
Troposphere 5

Ultraviolet radiation 16-17, 28
Unleaded petrol 13
Uranium 21
USA 28

Water 5, 6, 18, 29
Weather 24-25
Whale 6
Wind turbines 21